INTRODUCTION

The operating areas of the three companie
slice of the East Midlands. Barton with ı
and Leicestershire routes, Midland Gener:
mining and heavy urban areas of Derbysh
finally Mansfield District Traction (M
Nottinghamshire. Both Midland Genera........ ....
operating umbrella of the Wellglade Group. MGO in 1972/1976 and Barton
in 1989. For many years both MGO and MDT were sister companies within
the Balfour Beatty Group and then the British Transport Commission Group.
Buses were frequently loaned or transferred between both companies, until
the formation of the National Bus Company in 1968. The photos of all three
companies buses are in no date order. Alan Oxley's definitive histories of
Barton & MGO are strongly recommended.

Acknowledgements

Once again I am grateful for permission to use the photographs of the late
Colin F White from his son Rod. There are a few photos from my own
camera. My thanks also go to Paul Chambers for providing further
information and to my wife Gill for the hours spent looking at the PSV
Circle books for information and relating it to me for typing. Any errors are
the fault of the author.

Copyright - Alan Hiley
Derby, Summer 2022

A Commissioned Publication Printed by

MOORLEYS
Print, Design & Publishing
info@moorleys.co.uk • www.moorleys.co.uk

BARTON

Over many decades, Barton were well known for not only running a very successful bus and coach business but for their innovative experimental work with many types of bus. Lengthening chassis on early Daimlers, Chevrolets and Lancias. Swapping bodies and rebodying many types of vehicles, even cutting up two chassis and marrying one front half to the rear half of the second chassis. Their fleet was always of enormous interest to bus enthusiasts with the intake of new and many second hand vehicles. Their immaculate livery was known throughout the East Midlands and far beyond. In 1989 Barton was taken over by Trent Motor Traction Ltd. The vehicles were transferred to Barton Buses (Derby) Ltd.

Seen below basking in the sun at the Nottingham Area Bus Society (NABS) at Ruddington is preserved Leyland PD1 with Duple bodywork, JVO 230 awaiting its adverts to be applied. *Photo Alan Hiley*

945 MRR is at Derby Bus Station on 17th July 1962 working the X42 Nottingham Express. AEC Reliance with a Yeates 43 seat body, new in 1962. Sold in 1974 to the Arlington Motor Co Ltd in Cardiff, finally withdrawn in May 1978.

BVO 453 1936 Leyland LT7 Duple DP37F body. Seen in 1950s Huntingdon Street, Nottingham. Eventually used as a store shed by Barton Transport from July 1961 and scrapped by August 1963.

Leyland Tiger A618 ATV with Plaxton C53F body, seen on 2nd February 1984 at Leyland's depot at Aspley. New in 1983 and sold in July 1989, it sadly was burnt out at Blackpool Coach Station in June 2000.

E646 DAU a DAF with Plaxton C53F body, new in 1988 seen at Derby 28th July 1989 working the Llandudno service. It was withdrawn and sold to Sealandair Coaching in Bangor NI in May 1994. Only five years old. Scrapped in 2000 after an accident.

958 PRR AEC Regent V with NCME body, one of a batch of six delivered in 1963. Seen ready to work route 5 from Derby in 1965. A rear view also showing the advert for travel to Yarmouth. Sold to E Beckett, a dealer in Carlton in 1977 and scrapped by them in the same year.

960 PRR AEC Regent V with NCME, 70 seat full fronted body from the same batch new in 1963, seen at Derby Bus Station on 8th August 1973 on route 5 to Nottingham. Scrapped in August 1977.

BVO 456, one of the 1936 batch, it was re-bodied by Duple with a C39F body in late 1948. Seen in Mount Street, Nottingham. Again used as a store shed and scrapped in August 1963.

JRR 928 February 1948 LeylandPS1/1 had a Duple C35F body, parked in Mount Street Bus Station, equipped with radio, this was a classic Duple design. In late 1954, the chassis was reused for a Barton rebuild. Parked alongside is JRR 751 Leyland PD1A with a Duple body of 1948 vintage

Two views of CCU 276D Bedford VAL 14 with Duple 52 seat body, new in April 1966, acquired from Hall Brothers (South Shields) Ltd in February 1969. Seen parked in Derby Bus Station. Withdrawn in 1973, sold to B & J Coaches in Wales, withdrawn by them in June 1979. Did the driver have a grudge against the owner of the VW Beetle parking at the bus station?

Front and rear view of ERB 534T Leyland Leopard with Plaxton C53F body new in 1979 one of a batch of fourteen delivered during the year. Seen in Derby Bus Station when brand new. Transferred to Barton Buses Derby in July 1989 sold to Signet Travel in 1995. In preservation by February 2006 by J Phelan of New Ross Republic of Ireland.

HL 7432 Leyland TD4c, new in 1936 to West Riding Automobile Co Ltd, purchased by Barton in 1950, seen at Mount Street, Nottingham. Sold to Stansfield, a dealer in Nottingham December 1956.

KAL 150, one of eight Leyland PS1/1 delivered in 1948 with Duple C39F bodies, parked at Mount Street, Nottingham showing the lines of Barton coaches. Withdrawn in October 1965 and sold in February 1966 to the Rev Patchett at the Methodist Church, Netherfield. There are no further records of it.

Another of the 1948 intake was KAL 380 Leyland PS1/1 with a C39F Duple body, parked in Mount Street, Nottingham. In 1958, the body was scrapped and the chassis re-used as a Barton rebuild.

This atmospheric scene at Huntingdon Street bus station shows KAL 683 1949 Bedford OB with a Duple C29F body - did it really go to Norway? Fitted with a Perkins Diesel engine in October 1952. Following accident damage, it was scrapped in October 1959.

Standing amongst a fine selection of Barton double deckers at Mount Street is LNN 968, a 1950 Commer Avenger with a Churchill C34F body. Sold in July 1955 passing through many owners and last licenced in 1963.

Mount Street was a favourite place for Colin White's photographs. 1949 saw the arrival of KNN 254, a Leyland PD1A with a Duple 55 seat body. Sold in 1972 to a dealer in Bolton, moved on to at least seven others for preservation and currently housed at the Nottingham Area Bus Society at Ruddington.

Leyland Leopard with Plaxton C53F body XRR 623M, new in 1973. Parked at Trent Central Works, Uttoxeter New Road, Derby in October 1990 when its last licenced expired, it was used for spares.

UVO 128S, new to Trent in 1977, Leyland Leopard with Duple body painted in Barton livery in 1990, seen on 6th August 1992 in the Old Market Square, Nottingham. Withdrawn in 1994.

Ilkeston, where Barton had a depot for many years. PTV 584X 1981 Plaxton bodied Leyland Leopard, one of a batch of ten. Sold in April 1996 to Silverdale Tours. Scrapped in September 2004.

PTV 591X from the same batch, also in Ilkeston on 21st March 1982. Sold in 1996 passing through various operators and ending its life with Nottingham Heritage Vehicles for preservation, being scrapped in July 2008.

A colour photograph of PTV 591X in Ilkeston Market Place, 21st March 1982.

1961 saw the arrival of 861 HAL, a Dennis Loline III with a specially ordered NCME ultra low overall height of 12ft 5.5in. In Derby, 1st August 1973. Still in ownership of the Barton Treasured Vehicle Collection in 2022.

VVO 658L, a 1973 Leyland Leopard with Plaxton Body, seen in Derby, 14th July 1984 on route 5C. Acquired by Abbotts of Leeming North Yorkshire, September 1995, withdrawn by them in August 1996.

New in 1948 was JRR 930 Leyland PD1A with Duple lowbridge 55 seat front entrance body. Seen at Huntingdon Street Nottingham, ready to work service 14 to Ruddington. Retained by Barton Transport November 1973 and to Barton Cherished Vehicle Collection c1990, still owned by them in January 2009.

Leyland Leopard GNN 214N has broken down in Derby Bus Station on 21st December 1977 and is being rescued by the Scammell breakdown truck. GNN was sold to Bestwick's Coaches, Tibshelf in 1994 then passed to Camms of Nottingham in April 1998 and went to McIntyre, a dealer in Nottingham and was scrapped in March 2002.

NAS 624 AEC Matador Breakdown Truck, formerly Q957 AVO, but operated on trade plates 832AL.

Transferred to Barton Buses Derby Ltd in July 1989. Re-registered NAS 624 in October 2002. Seen here in preservation.

HAL 656, seen at Trent Station on 25th January 1948 when it was just a year old, was a 1947 Leyland PS1 with a Duple C32F body. Sold in 1949, passing through many owners and finally scrapped in June 1957.

HL 9057 was new to West Riding Automobile Co Ltd Wakefield in February 1939, new to Barton in 1949. Leyland TD5c with 48 seat Roe body. Re-seated by Barton to 55 seats before entering service. Scrapped in June 1960.

861 HAL Dennis Loline III seen at Ruddington on 30th October 1994. Showing a rear view, of which not many bus photographers generally take photos. Ruddington is now the home of the Nottingham Area Bus Society.

960 PRR AEC Regent V, new in 1963, with NCME FL37/33F body in Derby 8th August 1973. Sold to Bedlington Luxury Coaches Northumberland in 1974 and scrapped by August 1977.

903 LRR BTD2 chassis rebuilt from former Yorkshire Woollen District Leyland PD2/1 HD 7832, given NCME body in 1961, sold in 1975 to a dealer in South Anston, sold to Rosemary Coaches, Terrington St Clement, Norfolk, withdrawn in March 1976. Seen here in 1965 in Nottingham.

A617 ATV a 1983 DAF MB with a Plaxton C53F, seen at Derby Bus Station 11th April 1988. Withdrawn in August 1989 after only six years and sold to Skills Nottingham then sold in August 1990 to Stephensons of Tholthorp, North Yorkshire, used for spares and scrapped by October 2007.

B623 JRC, new in April 1985, DAF MB with Plaxton C53F body, seen on the 14th October 1989 in the Wardwick, Derby en-route to Blackpool to see the illuminations? Sold in 1997 passing through several operators and scrapped in July 2009.

Believed to be EK 7260, a Leyland bodied Leyland TD1, new November 1929 to Wigan Corporation, it entered service in 1947 after being rebuilt by Nudd of Chilwell. It was severely damaged after an accident at Spondon in April 1947 and then scrapped.

This poor quality photograph shows HL xxxx one of a batch purchased from West Riding Automobile Co Ltd as double deckers. Five of the batch were modified and re-seated to DP32 by Nudd Brothers & Lockyer of Kegworth in 1950. Seen at Mount Street Nottingham.

XRR 612M, new in 1973, Leyland Leopard with 53 seat Paxton body. Seen in Derby on 20th April 1989 on X42 express. It was scrapped in August 1994 at a Yorkshire breakers yard.

Leaving the passengers in no doubt where to board and alight is 966 RVO, a 1963 Bedford VAL 14 which carried a Yeates DP50D body. Sold in 1975 to Connor & Graham of Easington of East Riding. It went into preservation in 1985 and is still preserved today. Seen at the Peak Rail Rally Rowsley in 2019. *Alan Hiley*

A superb shot of XVO 787, new in 1958 Leyland PS1/B with NCME 61 seat body, seen at Derby 1st August 1973. Sold to Ensign Bus Co Hornchurch in November 1974. Then to Jones of Jacksonville, Florida, USA by November 1975. No Further records.

FTO 539V 1979 Leyland Leopard with Plaxton 53 seat body, seen outside Trent Central Works on 17th October 1989 just after Trent took over Barton. Sold in 1995 to Manor House Furnishers of Ilkeston as a mobile exhibition unit, then to Midland Fleet Maintenance by May 1999.

KAU 565V, a 1980 Leyland Leopard with Plaxton 53 seat body. In Derby on 13th March 1995 ready to work route 34 to Castle Donington. Withdrawn in 1996, sold to a dealer in Nottingham, eventually went to Ireland and was scrapped by June 2005.

Barton at the Celanese Works Spondon Derby

Photographs taken by the late Peter Taplin

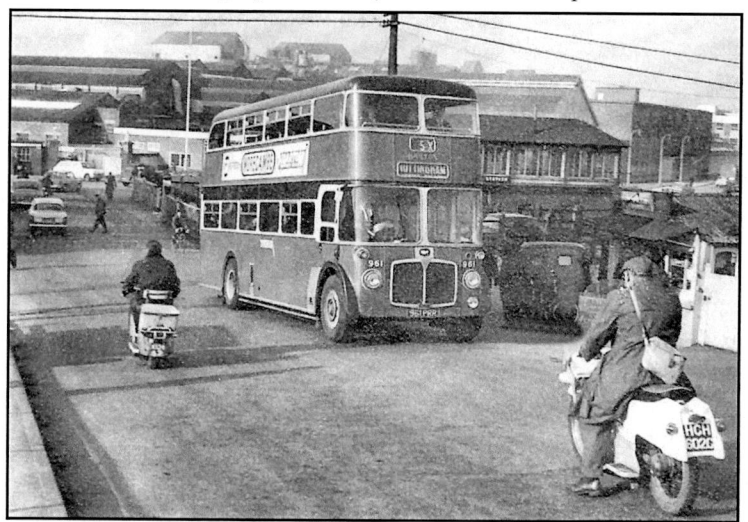

961 PRR AEC Regent V, new in 1963 NCME 70 seat body, seen leaving the huge Celanese works on 13th May 1966 after just crossing the railway line at Spondon Station, heading for Nottingham on the 5X service. Withdrawn in April 1977.

CNW 908 1935, ex Leeds City Transport, acquired in 1951. AEC Regent with Roe body at the Celanese Works with a Trent AEC and a Barton Leyland. Withdrawn in May 1956.

BARTON BUSES AT RUDDINGTON

There are now several Barton buses preserved and garaged at the Nottingham Area Bus Society (NABS) at Ruddington, Nottinghamshire. A hard working group of volunteers is dedicated to the aims of keeping the Barton fleet and vehicles firmly in the memory of bus enthusiasts, local folk and the travelling public who remember Barton buses with affection. The following photographs were taken by the author over several running days and show the hard work carried out by volunteers, not only with vehicle restoration but improving the garage facilities to a high standard.

The new garage almost complete showing the Felix Bedford, a Barton Leyland & AEC and an MGO Bristol MW. The majority of work was carried out by the team of volunteers lead by Paul Chambers.

A fine line up of Barton buses at the running day in July 2019.

JVO 230 1948 Leyland PD1A Duple 55 seat body, went into preservation in 1972 in Colchester, went onto other preservationists and now resides at Ruddington.

KNN 254 1949 Leyland PD1A (see page 11).

Two more photographs of KNN 254 showing the depth of work being carried out in preservation.

These photographs show both front and rear views of the Duple body which carried an almost coach-like interior.

Barton Line Up 2019 on a running day.

It was on a Sunday that the sign writer came to call (on the left).

Below, it's not a Barton bus but a Felix of Stanley, near Ilkeston, which is owned and has been renovated at Ruddington by Paul Chambers with help from his father, John, who was Bodyshop Manager at both MGO and Trent.

618 KRA was a 1959 Bedford SB1 with a Yeates Europa C41F body. Sold in June 1969. Purchased from Fowler Holbeach Grove.

MANSFIELD DISTRICT TRACTION

MDT was formed in September 1932 , its forerunners in Mansfield were the Mansfield & District Light Railway Company and the Mansfield & District Tramways Ltd. MDT, unlike other East Midland bus companies, did not acquire that many local operators. The Ebor Bus Company was acquired in 1950 with 23 vehicles, the firm of Bevan and Barker Red Bus Co in 1957 and Wains Coaches Ltd in 1960. The MDT livery was largely green and cream with some coaches and dual purpose vehicles painted in cream with black window surrounds. The management of MDT passed to the East Midlands Motor Services in 1976. After the advent of the National Bus Company, the livery became the standard NBC green.

My only slight involvement with MDT was when working as a relief garage foreman for Trent in the early 1980s. I carried out duties in that capacity at both Westgate and Sutton Road.

Mansfield Station, 27th July 1973, is the setting for 372 RNN Bristol MW6G/ECW C39F, new in 1963 looking very smart with translucent roof panels waiting to depart to Berryhill. Withdrawn in 1975 with no further details.

375 RNN 1963 Bristol FLF6G / ECW 70 seat body, new in 1963, in Mansfield 27th July 1973 heading to Langwith. Transferred to EMMS in 1976, by November 1980 it was sold to C F Booth, Rotherham for scrap.

FNN 750 AEC Regent / Weymann 52 seat body, new in 1939 and seen at an unknown location. Sold to W North Ltd of Leeds unknown date. Sold to Bowland of Wakefield by 1956.

CAL 199 AEC Regal / Weyman 31 seat body, new in 1936, is at Portland Square Sutton c1950. Fitted with an AEC 7.7 litre diesel engine during the 1940s. Disposal date unknown.

CVO 766 1937 AEC Regal /Weymann DP35F also in Portland Square Sutton in the 1950s. March 1954 sold to A Rhodes (dealer), Cardale Garage, Nottingham.

DAL 306C and DAL 308C, both from a batch of 1965 Bristol FLF6G /ECW 70 seat bodies, seen at Westgate, Mansfield, both on route 7 to Langwith. 306C passed through many owners finally becoming a static café by 2014 in France. 308C was scrapped by June 1982. Not such an interesting after life.

DRR 677 1938 AEC Regent /Weymann 56 seat body. Sold to AMCC Ltd of London by December 1955. There are no further details.

DRR 737 AEC Regent / Willowbrook 52 seat body. New to the Ebor Bus Co of Mansfield in November 1937. Ebor Bus Co was taken over by Mansfield District by March 1950. It is seen outside the Portland College in Westgate, Mansfield, with the EMMS garage in the background, also with a Trent AEC Regent behind. Went to Mather Bros Haulage Ltd, Chesterfield, as a lorry at an unknown date.

EVO 87 1939 AEC Regent/Weymann 56 seat body. Seen in an unknown location. Sold by August 1955 to an unknown buyer.

GNN 207 1944 Guy Arab II / Strachan 56 seat body seen in Queen Street, Mansfield, c1950, carrying an advert for CWS goods. Disposed of by January 1960 to G H Groves & Sons Ltd (Dealer) of London.

GRR 879 1946 AEC Regal/Duple DP35F body, acquired from Ebor in 1950. Transferred to MGO in 1955 and became a snowplough and was sold for scrap to Fisher & Ford of Carlton by August 1968.

JVO 933 1948 AEC Regent III / Weymann 56 seat body one of a batch of twenty eight seen in Portland Square, Sutton. Disposal date not known.

C328 HWJ 1985 Leyland ONLXB/1R/ECW 77 seat body in Derby Bus Station, 31st December 1989, in a drab green livery and the black back panel does little to enhance it. A lot brighter is the new Court House in the background.

BAU 179T, a 1979 Bristol VRT with 74 seat ECW body in Chesterfield on 23rd October 1991 carrying an advert for Mansfield Ales.

FNN 159D is a 1966 Bristol FLF6G with an ECW 70 seat body, 2nd October 1973, photographed outside Sutton Road Garage, Mansfield. It was transferred to EMMS in July 1976, then passing through numerous operators and exported to the USA in 1983, finally converted to a partial open top bus with the Cannery Co, Sumner, Washington in 2005.

HRR 242 was acquired from the Ebor Bus Co in 1950. 1948 AEC Regent III with a Brush 56 seat body in Mansfield c1950. A sticker in the nearside window says Operating Ebor Services. Its disposal date is unknown.

JVO 951, new to Mansfield District in January 1948, AEC Regent III 56 seat Weymann body. Seen picking up passengers on a wet, slushy winter's day in 1950 on service 101 to Woodhouse. It was transferred to the Nottinghamshire & Derbyshire Traction in 1953 and sold to Midland General in January 1965. The disposal date could be 1967 but it is not confirmed.

KAL 697 AEC Regent III with Brush 56 seat body, new to Ebor Bus Co Ltd in June 1949. Sold to MDT in 1950. In Westgate, Mansfield with two other Ebor buses. Sold in 1968. Seen below in Portland Square, Sutton, now in Mansfield livery.

JVO 950, new to MDT in 1948 AEC Regent III 56 seat Weymann body, parked in Portland Square, Sutton. Transferred to Notts & Derby in 1953, transferred again to MGO in 1965. Sold for scrap to Hartwood Finance Ltd, Birdwall, a dealer in March 1968.

JVO 943, another of the 1948 batch of AEC Regent IIIs with Weymann body, in another winter scene at Portland Square, Sutton. Transferred to Notts & Derby in 1953. Disposal was in 1967.

FNN 745 1940 AEC Regal with Weymann 35 seat body in Portland Square, Sutton, a favourite spot for Colin White's photographs. Transferred to MGO in November 1954 and became a snowplough. Sold in April 1966.

KRR 272 1949 AEC Regal III Weymann body in Portland Square, Sutton c 1949. Transferred to MGO in 1958 and sold for scrap to Dennis Higgs & Son, a dealer of Monk Bretton by October 1965.

Seen at an unknown location promoting either holidays or excursions, as can be seen by the boards at the front of the bus is KRR xxx. What is known is that it is an AEC Regal III with a Weymann body.

909 MRB, a Bristol FS6G ECW body, new to MGO in 1960, transferred to MDT parked at Sutton Road Garage in July 1973. It went to the NBC Disposal Centre, Bracebridge Heath, in November 1976. The rear view of 911 MRB can be seen.

Another Ebor vehicle, new in 1947, HAL 841 AEC Regent ECW, 56 seat body, sold to MDT in 1950. Parked in Westgate, Mansfield. Finally sold to East London Traders for scrap in December 1960.

SRB 64F 1967 Bristol FLF6G ECW 70 body, seen at Sutton Road Garage in July 1973. Sold in 1980, exported to Switzerland in 1987. Then came back to the UK in 1991 before going to Monnickendam in the Netherlands in 2009 and licenced as a 28 seat vehicle in December 2017. A far cry from Mansfield and District.

A rear view of TRB 583F, a 1968 Bedford VAM 70 Duple C41F body on 21st October 1973, Sutton Road. Transferred to MGO and returned to MDT in 1971. Sold by July 1976 and withdrawn by G R Vale Patricroft by 1981.

JNU 991D, new to MGO in 1966 Bristol MW6G ECW 44 seat body, transferred to MDT in April 1968, is parked at Mansfield Station in July 1973 in NBC green livery. Sold to Ensign Buses, a dealer, in 1978, sold to a construction company in Kinross in May 1978 and finally went to Shetland at an unknown date.

PSEUDO MANSFIELD DISTRICT TRACTION

By 1976, MDT had been totally absorbed into East Midlands Motor Services. The two photographs on this page are of Leyland Tigers with Alexander bodies. Neither of them were ever owned or worked for MDT, the top photo shows A41XHE wearing green 'Mansfield & District' livery at East Markham en-route to Doncaster on 28th March 1989. Below is seen A42 XHE in Mansfield on 6th June 1991 wearing the Stagecoach 'Mansfield & District' livery.

The ubiquitous Leyland National, foisted upon all NBC subsidiaries without a 'by your leave.' An unidentified National of 'Mansfield & District' is seen here at New Mills on 14th August 1989.

The lovely Derbyshire village of Crich is the setting for EKW 616V, a Leyland National 2 on route 140 to Alfreton on 5th September 1990. On the extreme left is a coach of Dunn Line.

BNU 671G Bristol LH6L ECW 45 seat body, new to MDT in 1969. Parked at Mansfield Station on a sunny day. Went to EMMS by July 1976. Sold to D Robinson of Carlton, a dealer, January 1980.

VO 8574 1932 AEC Regent Weymann 54 seat body. Sold to Balfour Beatty Co Ltd Newark for use at Staythorpe Power Station in 1948. Last licence expired December 1950. 14 of the same batch went to the power station. 8574 seen here after sale.

243 MNN 1962 Bristol FLF6G with ECW 70 seat body. Transferred to EMMS July 1976. Exported to the USA April 1980. Operated at the Tinker Air Force Base in Oklahoma by 1986. Converted to run on natural gas April 2004. Would gas improve a usually Gardner smoking engine?

SRB 60F Bristol FLF6G ECW 70 seater body, new in 1967 en route to Huthwaite with the crew having a chat. Exported to Florida at an unknown date and sold to Travelways in Chicago in 2000.

AAL 104B seen in 1976 at Mansfield garage was a 1964 Bristol FLF6B with ECW body. Sold to Norths (dealer) in 1978, passing through various operators before being scrapped in Wakefield in 1986.

MIDLAND GENERAL OMNIBUS CO

1922 saw the creation of the Midland General Omnibus Co. Over the next few decades, the company took over many local bus companies and one man bands. The main routes of operation were the heavy industrial areas of Derbyshire and Nottinghamshire. MGO operated many types of vehicles in the early days but, under the umbrella of the British Transport Commission (BTC), the fleet was later standardised on vehicles of the Bristol marque, often transferring or loaning vehicles to sister BTC company Mansfield District Traction and vice versa. In 1972, the National Bus Company decreed that MGO would be absorbed in the Trent Motor Traction fleet with ten vehicles transferred in 1972 and the remainder in 1976. The fleet, with its well turned out livery of dark blue and cream, gradually disappeared into the drab NBC poppy red, the MGO badge also vanished. The Colin White MGO photos were taken between the late 1940s and the late 1980s. Alan Oxley's history of MGO is recommended.

Below is 529 VRB, a 1962 Bristol FLF6B with 60 seat ECW body, seen at Cotmanhay on a rally in September 1985.

CRA 662 1936 AEC Regal Weymann 32 seat body, seen somewhere on tour. Rebuilt by MGO in 1954 and sold to A Rhodes, a dealer, in 1959 and passed onto Gunthorpe Gravels as a staff bus by October 1959.

DRA 160 1937 Leyland TS7 with Weymann DP35F body, seen in the old Bus Station at Alfreton in company with Naylor and Trent vehicles, both AEC Regents. DRA 160 was sold to Lansdowne Luxury Coaches Ltd, London, at an unknown date.

FRB 715 in Portland Square was a 1939 Leyland TS8 with Weymann DP35F body. Sold to A Camm of Nottingham in November 1958 and withdrawn for scrap in October 1959.

JRB 127 1946 AEC Regal Duple C35F body is seen alongside other AECs and Leylands at the Bakewell Show, 1950. JRB was sold in April 1960 to Nottingham City Council Education Committee.

JRB 131 1947 Leyland PS1 with Duple DP35F body, seen in Doncaster on a private hire in July 1948.

Sold to an unidentified owner in Nottingham by July 1960.

JRB 132 was the second of two Leyland PS1s purchased in 1947. Seen here in 1950. Sold to Machin of Surfleet Bank, Holland District, Lincolnshire by December 1960.

KRB 81 AEC Regent with Weymann 53 seat body, new in 1947, seen in Mansfield on route D1 to Chesterfield. Sold to North, a dealer, in February 1964 and sold to Dennis Higgs & Son, Monk Bretton, by July 1964.

MRB 30 1948 AEC Regent III Weymann 56 seat body, one of a batch of 15, again seen in Mansfield. There is no known record of its disposal. Advertising Spartona non alcoholic drink.

1384 R 1964 Bristol RELH6G ECW 51 seat body, parked up at Meadow Road, Derby, possibly awaiting sale. Transferred to Trent in 1976, withdrawn in May 1977 and sold to T Rigley, a dealer, for scrap in August 1977.

527 JRA a Bristol LD6G new in 1959 seen outside Trent Central Works Derby in September 1976, still carrying the MGO logo, withdrawn in November 1976 and went to NBC Disposal Centre at Bracebridge Heath.

Two photographs of DNU 13C at Matlock, June 1973, wearing the cream and black coach livery of MGO on route E2 to Alfreton. Bristol MW6G of 1965 vintage with ECW body, one of a batch of 7 purchased in that year. It was exported to Iran in March 1978, along with three others of the same batch.

A fine shot of DNU 970, one of a batch of 25 AEC Regents with Weymann 52 seat bodies, seen in Portland Square, Sutton, c1950. Body was overhauled by Nudd Bros & Lockyer of Kegworth. Sold to G H Groves & Sons London for scrap in January 1958.

HRA 924 a 1943 Guy Arab 1 Weymann 56 seat body which was originally intended for Manchester Corporation, parked in Mount Street, Nottingham, c1950. Sold to Rhodes, a Dealer of Nottingham, December 1960 and passed to Mr Dorman at Bunny, January 1961.

FRB 211H Bristol VRT/SL6G, new in 1970 seen at Mansfield in July 1973 heading to Alfreton. Moved to Trent in October 1976 and repainted in the original blue & cream MGO livery in September 1985 for the 65th anniversary of the company. Withdrawn in June 1988 and went to the Birmingham & Midland Motor Omnibus Trust at Whythall in December 1988 for preservation.

SRB 541 a 1953 Bristol KSW6G, shown as new to Notts & Derby coming down a wet Bath Street, Ilkeston, on route A2 to Cotmanhay. Withdrawn in 1969 and sent for scrap in 1970.

Only 10 vehicles were purchased in 1950, a batch of AEC Regent III with Weymann 53 seat bodies. ONU 630 is one of the batch seen in Mansfield Garage c1950. Sold in 1968 to F W Schermahorn, Wilmington USA.

ONU 631 from the same 1950 batch is at Mansfield on service D1 to Chesterfield. Withdrawn in 1968 and exported to Mariemont Inn, Chicago and finally sold to the Chicago Motor Coach Co by 1985 and still owned by them in 1992.

BNU 674G at Matlock Bus Station a Bristol LH6L with ECW 45 seat body, new in 1969. Went to Trent in 1976, sold in 1980 and served many operators in Shropshire and Wales and was derelict by 1990 and scrapped by 1993.

Parked outside Sutton Road Garage Mansfield on 21st October 1973 is SRB 66F Bristol RESH6G ECW DP43F body, new in 1967 painted in the cream and black livery. To Trent in 1976, transferred to the ancillary fleet as a driver trainer vehicle by March 1980. Sent to the APT at Bracebridge Heath in 1981 and was scrapped by June 1981.

Portland Square Sutton sees a 1945 Guy Arab II with NCME body. JNU 373. It had a body overhaul by Bonds of Wythenshawe in 1955 and was sold to W North of Leeds in August 1962.

JNU 735 is parked outside the Mansfield Shoe Co waiting to depart on service C3 to Clay Cross. A 1946 Guy Arab II with a Strachan 55 seat body, it had a body overhaul by Bonds of Wythenshawe in 1953. Sold to A Rhodes, dealer, in October 1959 and finally A Gale of Holbeach in January 1960.

In Mount Street Bus Station on 23rd June 1948 when only a month old is KRB 97 a Leyland PS1/1 with a Saunders DP35F body.

This vehicle was sold to Nottingham High School in April 1962.

A poor quality photo of the late 1960s shows XNU 414 Bristol LS6G, new in 1955 with the ECW DP43F body. In April 1969, it was sold to Eastern Counties Omnibus Co in Norwich. Scrapped in January 1974.

Colin White took all too few photos of Notts & Derby trolleybuses. On this page and the next are two of those. NNU 233 1949 BUT 7611T Weymann 56 seat body. Seen in Nottingham on the A1 route to Ripley. Most of the batch were sold to Bradford City Transport in April 1953. NNU 233 entered service in 1953 with Bradford in a special Coronation livery.

Seen in King Street Nottingham is NNU 235 another of the same 1949 batch. Sold to Bradford in 1953, withdrawn in 1963 and sold to L Nutton, a dealer of Stairfoot, Barnsley, for scrap in March 1967.

FRB 209H Bristol RELL6G new in 1970 ECW 44 seat body, seen in MGO livery on route F1. Went to Trent in 1976, became a driver training vehicle *(see page 91)*. Sold to West Sussex CC Education Department in 1985 and was rebuilt as a 'Technology Bus' by the British School of Technology in Carlton 1985.

XRB 415L was one of the first Leyland Nationals to enter service with MGO. New in 1972 and seen on service B6. Sold to East Midlands Airport as an airside passenger carrier in 1984. Now in preservation with P Chambers at Ruddington *(see page 98)*.

In Alfreton Bus Station on 3rd April 1976 is TCH 275L a 1973 Bristol RELH6G ECW body in Trent livery but carrying MGO roof logo. Withdrawn in July 1989, passing through many other owners and scrapped in July 1996.

Matlock Bus Station is the setting for TCH 278L on 1st October 1973 when four months old being purchased in June 1973, a Bristol RELH6L /ECW. To Trent in 1976, sold to the Northern Bus Co in June 1990, sold on to two different dealers and scrapped in 1995.

Showing A4 Limited Stop Special is MRB 36 one of a batch of 15 purchased in 1948. AEC Regent III with 59 seat Weymann body. The location is unknown but the house behind has a fine bush growing up the front. Its disposal date is unknown as eight others of the same batch are also unknown.

We see many shots of nearside and offside fronts of buses but not a lot of rear views. This photograph taken in Hucknall on 15th April 1948 shows HRA 417, a 1942 Leyland TD7 with a Leyland body of 56 seats. It was originally intended for Western SMT at Kilmarnock. It was sold in 1959 to G H Groves & Sons Ltd, a London dealer. Two small children are attempting to climb the north face of the entrance steps!!

Alfreton Bus Station is the setting for ORB 247K, a 1971 Bristol RELL6G with a ECW 44 dual door body. Painted in the cream & black livery of later years. To Trent in 1976, withdrawn in 1983, sold to Norths of Sherburn in Elmet and scrapped in July of the same year.

TCH 279L is a Bristol RELH6L with the usual ECW DP49F body, new in 1973, seen at Sutton Road Garage, Mansfield on 21st October 1973. Withdrawn with accident damage in December 1988, sold to North's and was scrapped by December 1989.

448 SNU 1962 Bristol FSF6G, new to Trent in 1976 and scrapped in June 1978 & XRC 607M, a Bedford YRQ with Duple C41F body - one of 3 new in 1974 withdrawn by Trent after a short working life in 1978.

Parked at Meadow Road, Derby, ORB 576P, a 1976 Leyland AN68/1R, with ECW 76 seat body.

These were ordered by MGO and entered service with Trent but with MGO fleet names.

Seen at Trent Central Works on 12th February 1977 with Trent fleet names, TRB 568F Bristol FLF6G was new to Notts & Derby in 1968, transferred to MGO in 1971 and to Trent in 1976. Withdrawn in March 1979 and exported to America, eventually ending its life as a trailer in Jacksonburg, Florida, by December 1992.

SRB 71F at Meadow Road, Derby on 15th September 1979 is a Bristol FLF6G new to MGO in 1967 and transferred to Trent in 1976, withdrawn in October 1979 and sold for scrap in November 1979.

Midland General at the Celanese Works Spondon Derby

Photographs by the late Peter Taplin

Swinging into Megaloughton Lane at Spondon on 25th June 1966 is 526 VRB Bristol FLF6B ECW body, new in 1962, transferred to Trent in 1976 and withdrawn in December 1977, finally scrapped in March 1978.

On an empty Celanese car park on 29th June 1962 is JNU 680 Guy Arab II with Roe body, new in 1945. It was rebodied by ECW in 1955 and withdrawn in August 1968, sold to Fisher & Ford Dealers of Carlton.

TREE LOPPERS & TRAINERS

Many vehicles in the group, after a long busy service life, were converted for other duties - including becoming driver training vehicles, tree loppers and in some cases breakdown and towing vehicles.

518 JRA 1959 Bristol LD6G ECW body, transferred to the ancillary fleet in February 1976 and converted to a tree lopper. Seen in Derby Bus Station on 31st January 1980 having cleared all the trees at the Bus Station! Withdrawn in August 1981.

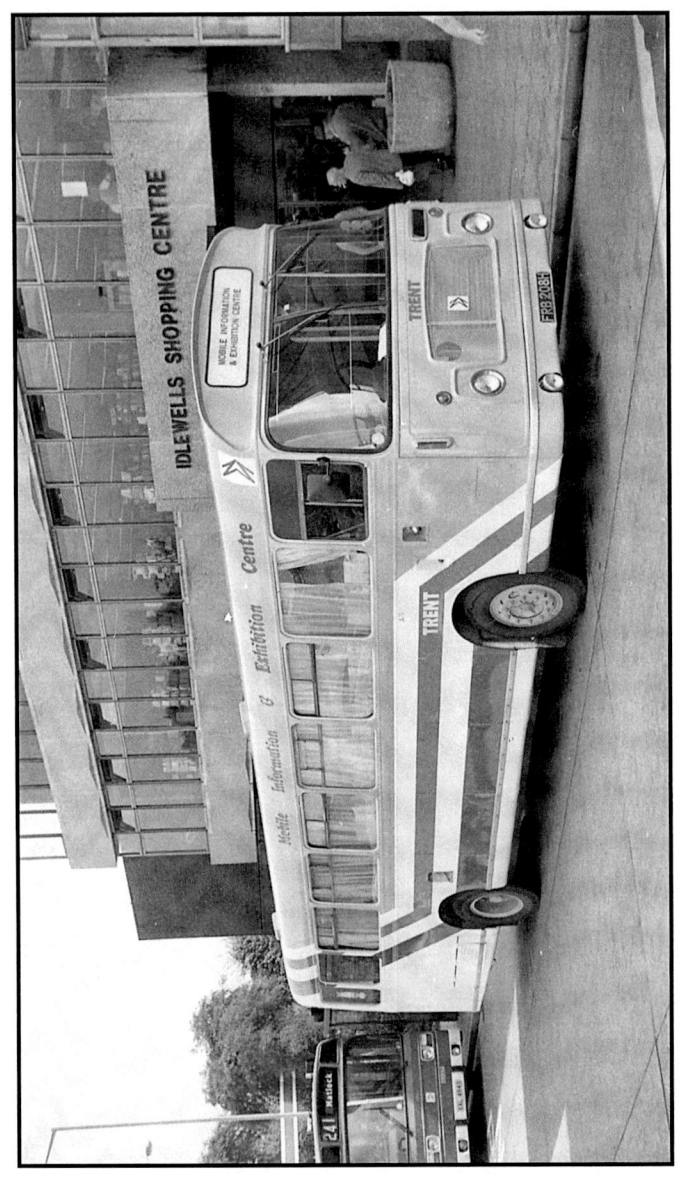

FRB 208H 1970 Bristol RELL6G, transferred to the ancillary fleet and converted to a mobile information and exhibition centre in October 1982. Converted to driver training bus in June 1983. Withdrawn in July 1987, passing through the hands of three preservation groups and now at the Nottingham Heritage Vehicles at Portland Road, Hucknall.

SRB 67F, new in 1967, a Bristol RESH6G at Meadow Road, July 1980. Converted to Driver Tuition bus in September 1979, withdrawn in March 1983 and scrapped in August 1984 by Martin's, a dealer of Middlewich, Cheshire.

FRB 209H 1970 Bristol RELL 6G, converted to driver training in September 1984, seen at Meadow Road on 23rd June 1985. (*For more details see page 78*).

RB 2309 AEC Regal with Willowbrook B32F body, new in August 1930 and one of the vehicles acquired from J G Severn & Co Ltd of Alfreton in March 1931. The business cost MGO £28,000. Severn traded as SMA (Severns Motor Auctions) The photo notes say 'after sale' the MGO garter is still on the side and the location is unknown. 2309 was sold to A Rhodes, a dealer in Nottingham and was scrapped in October 1950.

Parked at Meadow Road in June 1986 was XRB 420L, a 1973 Leyland National 44 seat dual door body. Sold to East Midlands Airport Authority in June 1984. Transferred to Stanstead Airport May 1995 and went back to EMA in September 1999 and back to Stanstead in May 2003.

Seen at Meadow Road on 3rd July 1989 was 529 VRB 1962 Bristol FLF6B. Withdrawn by Trent in 1978 after working for two jazz bands, it went into preservation in 1984 and was eventually exported to Switzerland in 1993.

KRR 255, new to Mansfield District in 1949, an AEC Regal III with Weymann DP35F body. Transferred to MGO in January 1958 and sold to J Peck of Mansfield Woodhouse for preservation in December 1967. It is still owned by him today. Seen at Brailsford on a road run on 25th September 1983.

DNU 20C, a 1965 Bristol MW6G ECW DP43F body new to MGO and transferred to MDT in 1968 it went to EMMS Chesterfield July 1976, sold to Cowley in December 1976 passing through several dealers, scouts and went into preservation in 1985 - now owned by Lynn Pestell who is seen here on a paint job at Ruddington where it is garaged.

NNU 447J, a 1971 Bristol RELL6G with the usual ECW B44D seat body. Withdrawn in February 1983, sold to East Midlands Airport Authority, sold back to Trent in 1989. Passed into preservation in 1989 and seen here at the Peak Rail Rally in 2019 in the ownership of Mark Bennett since June 1990.. Painted in cream and black showing both Mansfield District and Midland General fleet names. *(Alan Hiley)*

YNU 351G, a 1968 Bristol FLF6G ECW body with 70 seats. Transferred to Trent in 1976, withdrawn in 1979 and went to the MGO Preservation Group by January 1981. Now in the ownership of Arthur Webb since 1997. Seen at Brailsford on 25th September 1983.

Leyland National XRB 415L, seen at the Peak Rail Rally in 2019, now permanently residing at the Nottingham Area Bus Society (NABS) at Ruddington. (S*ee page 78).*

This photo caused a lot of head scratching. JAL 363, a Crossley with a Crossley body, was new to Baker of Warsop in 1949. Baker sold out to East Midlands Motor Service in February 1953. The photo was taken in Westgate, Mansfield and the bus has what looks like the MGO garter on the side. As it is a good photograph, I have decided to include it in this book. I have no further details.